LOCAL RED BOOK

CREWE NANTWICH

ELWORTH · SANDBACH · SHAVINGTON

G000297387

CONTENTS

Page Layout & Road Map   2
3 Miles to 1 Inch

Crewe Enlarged Centre   3
8 Inches to 1 Mile

Street Maps   4-14
4 Inches to 1 Mile

Index to Streets   15

Red Books showing the way

Every effort has been made to verify the accuracy of information in this book but the publishers cannot accept responsibility for expense or loss caused by an error or omission.

Information that will be of assistance to the user of the maps will be welcomed.

The representation on these maps of a road, track or path is no evidence of the existence of a right of way.

Street plans prepared and published by ESTATE PUBLICATIONS, Bridewell House, TENTERDEN, KENT. The Publishers acknowledge the co-operation of the local authorities of towns represented in this atlas.

Ordnance Survey This product includes mapping data licensed from Ordnance Survey® with the permission of the Controller of Her Majesty's Stationery Office.

www.ESTATE-PUBLICATIONS.co.uk

LEGEND

	Pedestrianized / Restricted Access
	Track
	Built Up Area
- - - - -	Footpath
	Stream
	River
Lock	Canal
	Railway / Station
●	Post Office
P P+	Car Park / Park & Ride
C	Public Convenience
+	Place of Worship
→	One-way Street
i	Tourist Information Centre
8 8	Adjoining Pages
	Area Depicting Enlarged Centre
	Emergency Services
	Industrial Buildings
	Leisure Buildings
	Education Buildings
	Hotels etc.
	Retail Buildings
	General Buildings
	Woodland
	Orchard
	Recreation Ground
	Cemetery

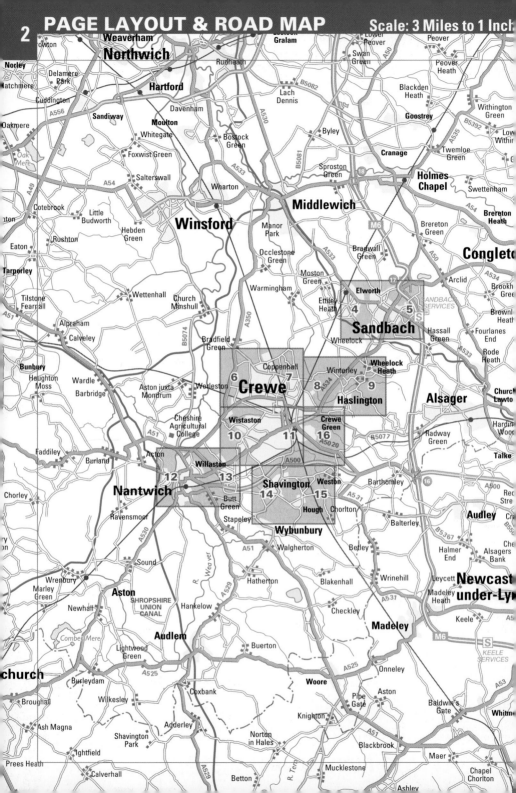

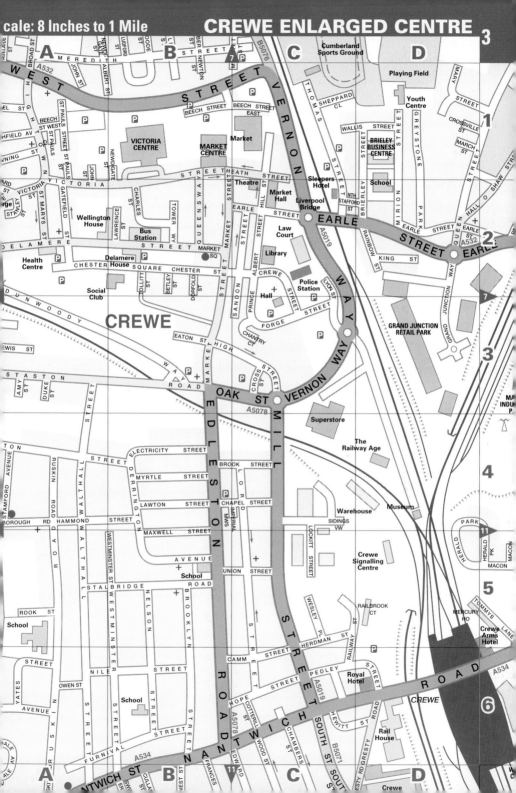

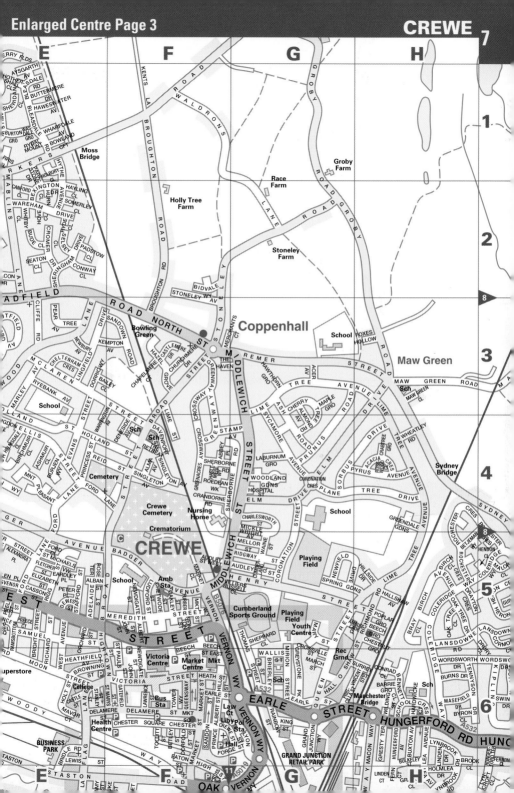

A B C D

1

2

3

4

5

6

Poplars Farm

Claylanes Farm

Foxholme Farm

Clayhanger Hall Farm

Tew Tree Farm

Brook House Farm

Bolton Farm

Sports Field

Cricket Ground

Thorneyfields Farm

Fowle Brook

Fox Covert

Works

Sch

Bradley Hall

Haslington

Sydney

Bradeley Abattoir

Hunters Lodge Hotel

Field Farm

The Brambles

Sch

Hall

School for the Disabled

Tollgate Farm

Halls

Crewe Green

MAW LANE

CLAY LANE

BY-PASS

MAW LANE

CLAY LANE

THE CLAY LANE

BRADELEY ROAD

HASLINGTON ROAD

HUNGERFORD ROAD

CREWE RD

GREEN RD

CREWE ROAD

NARROW LANE

B5077

A534

A532

Daughter Hill

nchester ropolitan iversity

FLOUR MILL WY

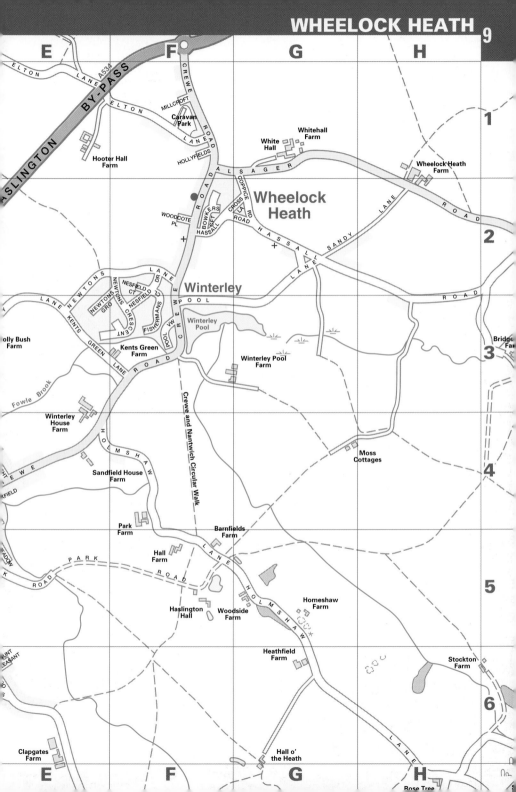

E F G H

1

Wheelock Heath

2

Winterley

3

4

5

6

ELTON LANE A534 BY-PASS

HASLINGTON

ELTON LANE

MILLCROFT

Caravan Park

CREWE ROAD

Hooter Hall Farm

HOLLYFIELDS

White Hall

Whitehall Farm

Wheelock Heath Farm

ALSAGER

COPPICE LA

CROSS LA RD

WOODCOTE PL

BOWKERS

HASSALL

HASSALL LANE

SANDY LANE

ROAD

ROAD

NEWTONS LANE

NESFIELD DR

NEWTONS GRO

NESFIELD CT

NEWTONS CRESCENT

FISHERMANS

CREWE ROAD

POOL

Winterley Pool

Kents Green Farm

KENTS GREEN LANE

Holly Bush Farm

Fowle Brook

Winterley House Farm

HOLMSHAW

Sandfield House Farm

CREWE

KFIELD

Crewe and Nantwich Circular Walk

Winterley Pool Farm

Moss Cottages

Bridge Fa

ROAD

Park Farm

PARK ROAD

Hall Farm

Barnfields Farm

LANE

HOLMSHAW

Homeshaw Farm

Stockton Farm

UNT EASANT

Haslington Hall

Woodside Farm

Heathfield Farm

Clapgates Farm

Hall o' the Heath

Rose Tree

E F G H

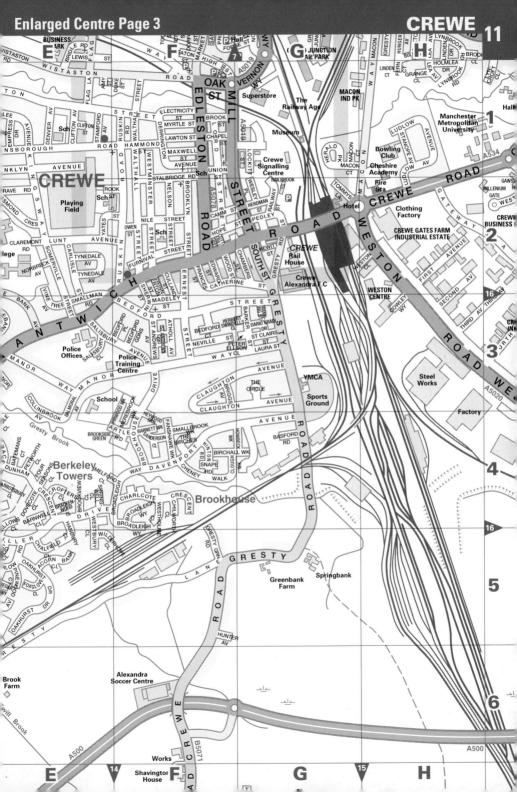

E   F   G   H

1

Manchester
Metropolitan
University

CREWE

Playing Field

MACON IND PK

Ludlow

Bowling Club
Cheshire Academy

CREWE BUSINESS

2

Police Offices

Police Training Centre

School

Berkeley Towers

Brookhouse

Superstore

The Railway Age

Museum

Crewe Signalling Centre

Fire Sta

Clothing Factory

CREWE GATES FARM INDUSTRIAL ESTATE

CREWE Rail House

Crewe Alexandra F.C

WESTON CENTRE

Hotel

Steel Works

Factory

16

3

THE CIRCLE

YMCA

Sports Ground

4

16

Greenbank Farm

Springbank

5

Brook Farm

Alexandra Soccer Centre

Works

Shavington House

A500

A500

6

E   F   G   H

Electricity
Myrtle St
Lawton St
Maxwell St
Union St

Oak St

Vernon Wy

Junction Rail Park

A full-page street map of Nantwich. Labels include:

Holly Farm, The Green, Police Dog Training School, Welshmens Lane, Henhull Hall, Home Farm, Beam Bridge, Nantwich By-Pass, A51, B5074, A500, Alvaston Business Park, Middlewich Road, Cricket Grnd, Cemetery, Willow Farm, Superstore, The Barony Employment Park, Works, Barony Park, The Barony, Kingsleyfield Farm, Playing Field, All Weather Pitch, Marina, Acueduct, Shropshire Union Canal, School, Snow Hill, Lode Water, Swimming Pool, Welsh Row, Weaver Water, Beam Water, Liby, Civic Hall, Health Centre, Fire Sta, Museum, Nantwich, Millstone, Crewe, London, A51, A534, Football Grnd, Reaseheath College, Penlington, Marsh Lane, Fields Farm, Brookfield Park, Green Lane Bridge, River Weaver, Shrewbridge, Baddington Lane, Park Road, Wellington Road, Nantwich View, Station, Hillfield, Jubilee, Brookfield Park, School, Audlem, Peter Destapleigh Wy, A531, Clonners, Thomas Av, School, Bishops Bridge, Shrew Bridge

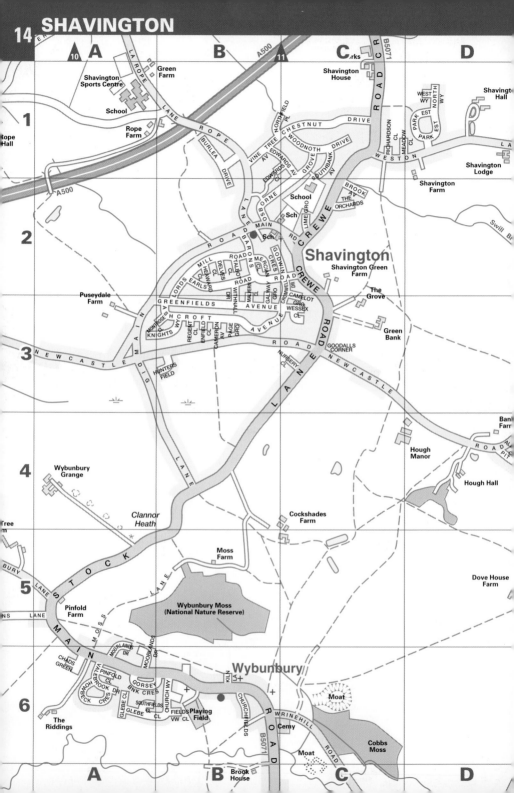

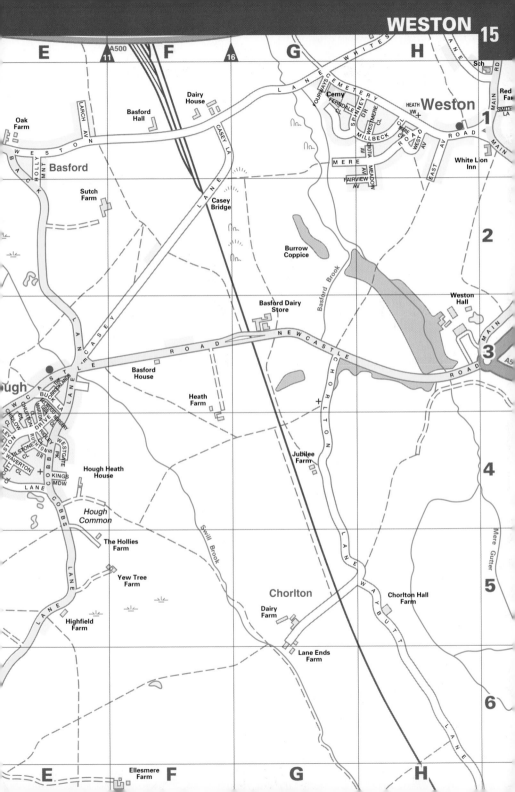

E   A500   11   F   16   G   H

Sch

Red Far

Weston

Oak Farm

WESTON BACK

HOLLY MNT

LARCH AV

Basford

Basford Hall

Dairy House

FOURWAYS LANE

CEMETERY

WHITES LANE

Cemy

FERNDALE CL

SPINNEY DR

WESTMERE CL

CLIFFE AV

HEATH VW

EAST AV

ROAD

MAIN RD

SMITH LA

CASEY LA

MILLBECK

WEST RD

CROFT

1

Sutch Farm

MERE

MERE AV

CROTIA AV

MEADOW

White Lion Inn

FAIRVIEW AV

Casey Bridge

Burrow Coppice

2

LANCASTER CASEY LANE

ROAD

Basford Dairy Store

NEWCASTLE

Basford Brook

Weston Hall

MAIN

3

A5

ugh

BUCK LA

SPRINGBANK

WICK

CHURCH MARTON NURSERY

RIDLEY

DRIVE

WESTGATE

CLOSE

WILSTONE CL

RUSHTONS

CLIFF

WAVERTON CL

KINGS MDW

DUCKOW

COBBS LANE

LANE

Basford House

Heath Farm

CHORLTON

Jubilee Farm

4

Hough Heath House

Hough Common

Hough Common

LANE

LANE

Swill Brook

Mere Gutter

5

The Hollies Farm

Yew Tree Farm

Chorlton

Dairy Farm

WAYBUTT

LANE

Chorlton Hall Farm

Highfield Farm

Lane Ends Farm

6

Ellesmere Farm

E   F   G   H

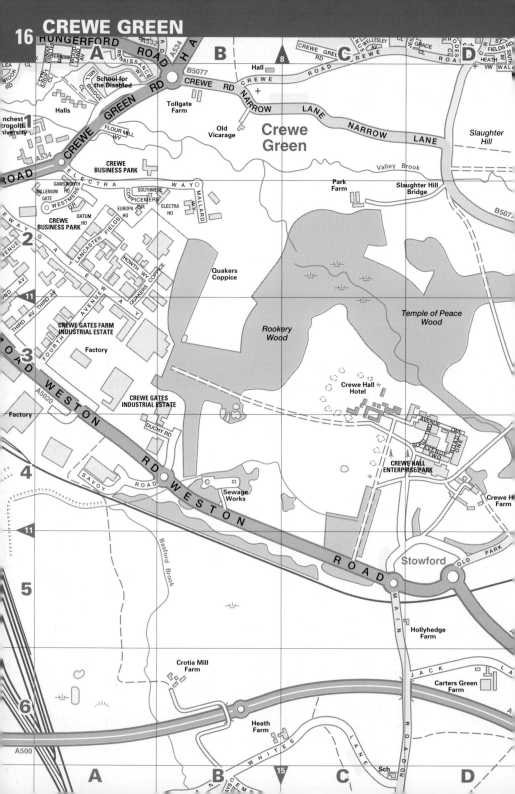

Map labels

A / **B** / **C** / **D** (column grid)
1 / **2** / **3** / **4** / **5** / **6** (row grid)

HUNGERFORD ROAD
A532
A534
CL Wellesley CL JES GRACE CL RHODES CL
CREWE GREE
CREWE
FIELDS CL
SCH
HEATH
WAL
ST
CREWE GREEN RD
B5077
Hall
8
CREWE RD
ROAD
School for the Disabled
RENAISSANCE
MILL BRIDGE
WOODCROFT CL
FERNBANK
Halls
Tollgate Farm
CREWE RD
NARROW
LANE
nchester tropolitan niversity
FLOUR MILL WY
Old Vicarage
CREWE
NARROW LANE
Crewe Green
Slaughter Hill
A534
CREWE GREEN RD
CREWE BUSINESS PARK
ELECTRA WAY
MALLARD
Valley Brook
Park Farm
Slaughter Hill Bridge
B507
GAWSWORTH
MILLENIUM GATE
WESTMER DR
HO
SOUTHMERE CT
COPPICEMERE
EUROPA CR
DATUM HO
COPPICEMERE
ELECTRA HO
LANCASTER FIELDS
HOWTH WY
QUAKERS COPPICE
Quakers Coppice
Temple of Peace Wood
CREWE BUSINESS PARK
THIRD AV
AVENUE
FOURTH
THIRD AV
SECOND AV
11
CREWE GATES FARM INDUSTRIAL ESTATE
Factory
Rookery Wood
Crewe Hall Hotel
Factory
WESTON ROAD
A5020
CREWE GATES INDUSTRIAL ESTATE
DUCHY RD
CREWE HALL ENTERPRISE PARK
AVENUE ONE
AVENUE TWO
ROAD ONE
SAVOY ROAD
WESTON RD
Sewage Works
Crewe H Farm
11
Basford Brook
WESTON ROAD
Stowford
OLD PARK
MAIN
Hollyhedge Farm
Crotia Mill Farm
JACK
LA
Carters Green Farm
ROAD
A500
Heath Farm
WHITES
LANE
ROAD
Sch

The Index includes some names for which there is insufficient space on the maps. These names are indicated by an * and are followed by the nearest adjoining thoroughfare.

Abbey Flds CW2 10 A4
Abbey Pl CW1 7 F4
Abbey Rd CW11 4 B3
Abbotsbury Cl CW2 11 E4
Abingdon Cl CW1 7 E4
Acacia Cres CW1 7 H4
Acacia Dr CW11 4 B2
Acer Av CW1 7 G3
Acorn Bank Cl CW2 11 E5
Acton Rd CW2 6 A5
Addison Cl CW2 10 C4
Adelaide St CW1 7 E5
Adlington Dr CW11 5 F2
Adlington Rd CW2 10 C1
Alban St CW1 7 E5
Albert St, Crewe CW1 3 A1
Albert St,
  Nantwich CW5 12 C2
Albion St CW2 10 D1
Alderley Cl CW1 5 F1
Aldersey Rd CW2 10 C1
Aldford Cl CW2 14 D4
Alexandra Pl CW1 7 E5
Allen Pl CW1 7 E5
Allman Cl CW1 6 C3
Alma Av CW1 7 F4
Almond Av CW1 7 G3
Alsager Rd CW11 9 F1
Alton St CW2 3 A4
Alvaston Rd CW5 12 C3
Alvaston Walk CW2 10 B2
Ambleside Cl CW2 10 B2
Ambuscade Cl CW1 7 G5
Amy St CW2 3 A3
Anderson Cl CW1 8 A5
Angelina Cl CW11 4 A2
Anvil Cl CW11 4 C6
Arderne Av CW2 10 C2
Ardleigh Cl CW1 6 C2
Arley Pl CW2 10 D4
Arley Walk CW11 4 A4
Armitstead Rd CW11 4 C5
Arnold St CW5 12 C2
Arran Cl CW2 10 A1
Artle Rd CW2 11 E4
Arundel Cl CW2 10 B4
Ash Gro CW5 12 C5
Ash Ho*,
  Brook Ct CW11 5 E3
Ash Rd CW1 7 G3
Ashcroft Av CW2 14 B3
Ashlea Dr CW5 13 H4
Ashley Mdw CW1 8 D4
Ashmuir Cl CW1 7 E4
Ashville Ct CW2 10 D5
Asquith Cl CW1 7 E4
Astbury Cl CW1 6 D3
Atholl Av CW2 11 F3
Attwood Cl CW1 8 D5
Audlem Rd CW5 12 C6
Audley St CW1 7 G5
Audley St West CW1 7 F5
Austen Cl CW11 4 A3
Avenue One CW1 16 D4
Avenue Two CW1 16 D4
Avon Dr CW1 8 A4
Aysgarth Av CW1 7 E1

Back La CW2 15 E1
Baddington La CW5 12 B6
Badger Av CW1 6 C4
Badgers Wood CW2 10 B3
Bailey Cl CW1 7 E3
Bailey Cres CW11 5 G3
Baker Cl CW2 10 D2
Balfour Cl CW1 8 D5
Balmoral Av CW2 11 E4
Balmoral Pl CW1 13 H4
Bankfield Av CW2 10 D5
Bannacks Cl CW5 13 G2
Barker St, Crewe CW2 11 G3
Barker St,
  Nantwich CW5 12 B4

Barlow Way CW11 4 D1
Barnabas Av CW1 6 C4
Barnato Cl CW1 6 C3
Barnes Cl CW1 8 D5
Barnett Walk CW2 11 F4
Barnwell Cl CW2 11 E4
Baronia Pl CW5 12 C3
Barons Rd CW2 14 B2
Barony Bldgs CW5 12 C2
Barony Ct CW5 12 C1
Barony Rd CW5 12 B1
Barrie Gro CW1 7 H6
Barrows Cl CW1 6 C2
Barthomley Cres CW2 6 A5
Basford Rd CW2 11 G4
Basset Cl CW5 13 H2
Batemans Ct CW2 11 E4
Bath St CW11 5 F3
Batherton La CW5 12 D6
Batterbee Ct CW1 8 D5
Bayley Rd CW5 13 G3
Beam Heath Way CW5 12 C1
Beam St CW5 12 B3
Beatty Rd CW5 12 B4
Beaumont Cl CW2 10 C4
Becconsall Cl CW1 6 D2
Becconsall Dr CW1 6 D2
Beckford Cl CW1 6 C2
Bedford Cl CW2 11 F3
Bedford Gdns CW2 11 F3
Bedford Pl CW2 11 F3
Bedford St CW2 11 F3
Beech Dr CW2 10 B2
Beech Gro, Crewe CW1 7 H5
Beech Gro,
  Sandbach CW11 5 F3
Beech St CW1 3 B1
Beech St East CW1 3 C1
Beech St West CW1 3 A1
Beech Tree Cl CW5 13 G3
Beechcroft Av CW2 11 E5
Belgrave Rd CW2 11 E2
Belle Vue Ter CW11 5 E3
Belmont Av CW11 4 D2
Beltony Dr CW1 6 D1
Bennett Cl CW1 7 H6
Bentley Dr CW1 8 A5
Berkeley Cres CW2 10 D4
Betchton Cl CW11 5 F2
Betchton Rd CW11 5 F6
Betjeman Way CW1 7 H5
Betley St CW1 3 B2
Bexington Dr CW1 7 E2
Bickley Cl CW2 15 E4
Bidvale Way CW1 7 F2
Billington Cl CW2 10 D2
Bilton Way CW2 6 B5
Binyon Way CW1 8 A6
Birch Av CW1 7 H5
Birch Cl CW1 7 H5
Birch Gdns CW1 5 F3
Birchin Cl CW1 12 D2
Birchin La CW5 12 D2
Birchmuir Cl CW1 7 E4
Birchwood Dr CW5 12 D3
Birtles Cl CW11 5 E2
Bishops Wood CW5 12 D6
Blackacres Cl CW11 4 C3
Blackthorn Cl CW2 10 D4
Blagg Av CW5 12 A4
Blake Cl CW2 10 C3
Blakemere Way CW5 4 C1
Bleasdale Rd CW1 7 E1
Blenheim Cl CW2 10 B4
Blenheim Pk CW1 4 D5
Boden Dr CW5 13 H4
Bodnant Cl CW1 6 D2
Bold St CW1 8 C6
Bollands Row*,
  Churches Ct CW5 12 C4
Bollin Cl CW11 4 B1
Bolshaw Cl CW5 6 D3
Bolt St CW11 5 E3
Booth Av CW1 7 G6
Boothsmere Cl CW11 4 C1
Borrowdale Cl CW2 10 B1
Boulton Cl CW11 5 F6
Bowen Cooke Av CW1 6 B2
Bowen St CW2 10 D1
Bowers Row CW5 12 B3

Bowkers Cft CW11 9 F2
Bowland Cft CW1 7 E1
Bowles Cl CW1 4 C3
Bowline Cl CW11 5 F6
Bowness Rd CW2 10 B1
Bowyer Av CW5 12 C3
Brackenwood Cl CW2 11 E4
Bradeley Hall Rd CW1 8 A4
Bradeley Rd CW1 8 C5
Bradfield Rd CW1 6 C1
Bradwall Rd CW11 4 D1
Bradwall St CW11 4 D2
Braermar Cl CW2 10 B4
Bramall Cl CW11 5 F1
Bramhall Rd CW2 10 B1
Brassey St CW5 13 F2
Brassey Way CW5 13 G3
Bray Cl CW1 7 H5
Brecon Way CW2 10 D5
Brereton Cl,
  Crewe CW2 10 B2
Brereton Cl,
  Sandbach CW11 5 F2
Brereton Dr CW5 12 D2
Briardale Cl CW2 10 C4
Brick Bank CW5 12 D3
Bridge Cl CW2 10 D5
Bridgemere Cl CW11 4 B1
Bridle Hey CW5 12 D6
Bridle Rd CW2 7 E6
Brierley St CW1 3 D2
Briggs Av CW2 11 F3
Bright St CW1 7 E6
Brindley Pk CW11 4 C6
Brine Rd CW5 12 C6
Broad St CW1 3 A1
Broadleigh Way CW2 11 F4
Brock Hollow CW11 4 B5
Bromley Cl CW1 6 C2
Brook Av CW2 14 C2
Brook Cl CW1 7 H6
Brook Ct CW11 5 E3
Brook St CW2 3 B4
Brook Ter CW11 4 D6
Brook Way CW5 12 C5
Brookdale Pk CW2 10 C1
Brookfield CW1 9 E4
Brookhouse Dr CW2 11 F4
Brookhouse Rd CW11 5 E3
Brookland Av CW2 10 C4
Brookland Dr CW11 5 G3
Brooklands Gro CW1 6 D4
Brooklyn St CW2 3 B5
Brookmere Cl CW11 4 B1
Brookside Grn CW2 11 E4
Brookview Cl CW2 11 E4
Broom St CW1 6 D4
Broughton La CW2 10 C3
Broughton Rd CW1 7 F1
Brown Av CW5 12 D5
Browning Cl CW11 4 A4
Browning St CW1 3 A1
Brownlees Cl CW2 10 D3
Brunner Gro CW5 13 E4
Buchan Gro CW2 10 D1
Buck La CW2 15 E3
Buckingham Cl,
  Crewe CW2 10 B4
Buckingham Cl,
  Nantwich CW5 13 H1
Bude Cl CW1 7 E2
Budworth Cl CW11 4 B2
Bulkeley St CW1 7 H6
Burgess Cl CW5 13 F4
Burjen Way CW1 7 E4
Burlea Cl CW2 6 B5
Burlea Dr CW2 14 B1
Burnell Cl CW5 12 D5
Burns Dr CW1 7 H6
Burton Gro CW1 7 E1
Butler Way CW5 12 C6
Buttermere St CW1 7 E1
Buxton Av CW1 7 H6
Byron Cl, Crewe CW1 7 H6
Byron Cl,
  Sandbach CW11 4 A3
Byron Walk CW5 12 B3
Byron Way CW2 10 C3

Caernarfon Dr CW2 10 B4
Calder Av CW1 8 A4

Caldwell Cl CW5 13 E5
Camelot Gro CW2 14 C3
Cameron Av CW2 14 B3
Camm St CW2 3 B6
Campbell Cl CW1 8 C5
Canford Cl CW1 7 E2
Capenhurst Av CW2 10 C1
Capesthorne Cl CW11 5 F1
Capesthorne Rd CW2 10 B2
Carisbrooke Cl CW2 10 B4
Carlisle St CW2 11 E2
Carrington Way CW1 6 D2
Carroll Dr CW2 10 C4
Carter Cl CW5 12 B3
Cartlake Cl CW5 12 A4
Cartwright Rd CW1 9 E4
Casey La CW2 15 E3
Casson St CW1 7 E5
Castle St, Crewe CW1 7 E6
Castle St,
  Nantwich CW5 12 B3
Castlemere Dr CW1 7 F3
Catherine St CW2 11 F2
Cavendish Rd CW2 6 B5
Cecil Rigby Cl CW11 5 E3
Cedar Ct CW5 13 H3
Cedar Gro CW5 13 E3
Cedar Way CW2 11 E5
Cemetery Rd CW2 15 G1
Cestria Cl CW11 4 A2
Chads Grn CW5 14 A6
Chadwicke Cl CW5 12 D4
Chalfield Cl CW2 11 E5
Chamberlain Ct CW1 8 D5
Chambers St CW2 3 C6
Chantry Ct CW1 3 C3
Chapel Row CW5 12 A3
Chapel St, Crewe CW2 3 B4
Chapel St,
  Sandbach CW11 5 E2
Chapel St,
  Wheelock CW11 4 D6
Chapelmere Cl CW11 4 B2
Chapelmere Ct CW1 7 F3
Charlcote Cres CW2 11 F4
Charles Ho*,
  Princes Ct CW2 10 C1
Charles St CW1 3 B2
Charlesworth Ct CW11 5 F3
Charlesworth St CW1 7 G4
Chartwell Pk CW11 4 D5
Chater Dr CW5 12 D5
Chatham Way CW1 8 C5
Chatsworth Cl CW2 10 D4
Cheerbrook Rd CW5 13 G5
Chell St CW1 7 E5
Cheltenham Cres CW1 7 E3
Cheney Walk CW2 11 F4
Cheriton Way CW2 10 D4
Cherrington Rd CW5 12 C6
Cherry Gro CW5 12 A4
Cherry Tree Rd CW1 7 G3
Chester Sq CW1 3 A2
Chester St CW1 3 B2
Chesterton Dr CW2 10 C3
Chesterton Gro CW11 4 A4
Chestnut Dr CW2 14 C1
Chestnut Gro CW1 7 H5
Chestnut Ho*,
  Brook Ct CW11 5 E3
Chetwode St CW1 7 F5
Cheyne Walk CW5 12 C6
Chidlow Cl CW2 15 E3
Chilworth Cl CW2 11 F4
Chorlton La CW5 15 G3
Christchurch Av CW2 10 D3
Christleton Av CW2 6 A5
Church La, Crewe CW2 10 B5
Church La,
  Nantwich CW5 12 C3
Church La,
  Sandbach CW11 5 H1
Church St CW11 5 E3
Church Vw CW1 8 D5
Church Way CW5 14 B6
Churches Ct CW5 12 C4
Churchfields CW5 14 B6
Churchmere Dr CW1 7 F3
Churchyard Side CW5 12 C3
Churton Cl CW2 15 E3
Circle Av CW5 13 H4

Clare Dr CW2 10 C3
Claremont Rd CW2 11 E2
Clarence Gro CW1 7 E5
Claughton Av CW2 11 F3
Clay La CW1 8 C1
Clayton Cl CW1 6 D3
Claytons Row CW5 12 C2
Clement Dr CW1 6 C3
Cliffe Rd CW1 7 E3
Clifford Gro CW1 8 C5
Clifton Av CW2 11 E1
Clifton Rd CW11 4 A2
Clifton St CW2 11 E1
Clonners Fld CW5 12 D4
Clough Walk CW2 11 F4
Cloverfields CW1 8 C6
Clyde Gro CW2 10 D1
Clydesdale Av CW2 10 D1
Cobbs La, Crewe CW2 15 E4
Cobbs La,
  Nantwich CW5 12 C1
Coldmoss Dr CW11 5 F4
Coleridge Way CW1 7 H5
College Flds CW2 10 D3
Colley La CW11 5 F4
Colleys La CW5 13 E1
Collinbrook Av CW2 11 E3
Collins St CW2 10 D1
Comberbach Dr CW5 13 E5
Condliffe Cl CW11 5 E3
Congleton Rd CW11 5 E3
Coniston Cl CW5 12 D2
Conrad Cl CW1 7 H6
Conway Cl CW1 7 E2
Cookesmere La CW11 4 C1
Coopers Opening CW11 5 E2
Cope Av CW5 12 A5
Copes La CW5 12 A4
Coppenhall Gro CW2 6 C6
Coppenhall Heyes CW2 6 D6
Coppenhall La CW2 10 A1
Coppice Cl CW5 13 G2
Coppice Rd,
  Nantwich CW5 13 G2
Coppice Rd,
  Sandbach CW11 9 G1
Coppicemere Dr CW1 16 A2
Cormorant Cl CW1 8 A5
Cornwall Gro CW1 7 E5
Coronation Cres,
  Crewe CW1 7 G4
Coronation Cres,
  Sandbach CW11 4 D4
Coronation St CW1 7 G5
Cotterill St CW2 3 C6
Cottons La CW11 4 D6
Coverdale Fold CW11 4 A4
Cowfields CW5 12 C3
Cowley Way CW1 11 H3
Cowper Cl CW2 10 C4
Crabmill Dr CW11 4 B2
Crabtree Gro CW1 7 H4
Cranage Rd CW2 10 D1
Cranborne Rd CW1 7 F4
Cranebrook Cl CW1 6 D2
Crestwood Cl CW2 11 E5
Crewe Bsns Pk CW1 16 A1
Crewe Gates Farm
Ind Est CW1 11 H2
Crewe Gates Fm
Ind Est CW1 16 A3
Crewe Gates
Ind Est CW1 16 A3
Crewe Green Rd,
  Crewe Green CW1 16 A1
Crewe Green Rd,
  Haslington CW1 8 C6
Crewe Hall
Enterprise Centre
CW1 16 D4
Crewe Rd, Crewe CW1 11 H2
Crewe Rd,
  Crewe Green CW1 8 B6
Crewe Rd,
  Nantwich CW5 12 D4
Crewe Rd,
  Sandbach CW11 4 C6
Crewe Rd,
  Shavington CW2 14 C2
Crewe Rd,
  Wheelock Heath CW11 9 F1

Crewe Rd,
Wistaston CW2 — 10 B5
Crewe St CW1 — 3 C2
Crofters Cl CW2 — 11 E4
Cromer Dr CW1 — 7 E2
Cromwell Ct CW5 — 12 C3
Cromwell Dr CW2 — 14 C3
Cronkinson Av CW5 — 12 C5
Cronkinson Oak CW5 — 12 C4
Cross La,
Sandbach CW11 — 5 F4
Cross La,
Wheelock Heath CW11 — 9 F2
Cross Rd CW1 — 8 D6
Cross St, Crewe CW2 — 3 C3
Cross St,
Haslington CW1 — 8 D6
Cross St,
Sandbach CW11 — 5 F4
Cross Wood St CW5 — 12 B3
Crosslands CW1 — 8 D6
Crossville St CW1 — 3 D1
Crossway CW1 — 7 F4
Crotia Av CW2 — 15 H1
Crown Bnk CW11 — 5 E3
Crown Dr CW11 — 5 F6
Culland St CW2 — 11 F2
Cumberland Av CW5 — 12 D2
Cumberland Cl CW1 — 7 G5
Cumbermere Dr CW11 — 4 B1

Dairy House Way CW2 — 10 C2
Daisy Bank CW5 — 12 A4
Daisybank Dr CW11 — 5 F3
Dale St CW1 — 6 D4
Dalton Ct CW1 — 4 B2
Dane Bank Av CW2 — 10 C2
Dane Cl CW11 — 4 B2
Dapplcheath Rd CW2 — 10 D3
Dario Gradi Dr CW2 — 11 G3
Darley Av CW2 — 10 D1
Darlington Av CW1 — 6 C4
Datum Ho CW1 — 16 A2
Davenham Cres CW2 — 10 C1
Davenport Av,
Crewe CW2 — 11 F4
Davenport Av,
Nantwich CW5 — 12 C2
Davenport Cl CW11 — 5 F1
Davenport St CW1 — 7 F4
Deadmans La CW5 — 13 E6
Dean Cl CW11 — 4 B1
Deane Ct CW5 — 13 E4
Deans La CW11 — 4 B3
Dee Cl CW11 — 4 B1
Delamere Cl CW11 — 4 C1
Delamere Rd CW5 — 12 C5
Delamere St CW1 — 3 A2
Delves Broughton Ct
CW1 — 14 B2
Delves Cl CW2 — 14 B2
Deneside Av CW1 — 7 F4
Denston Cl CW2 — 10 D3
Denver Av CW2 — 11 E1
Derby St CW1 — 7 E5
Derrington Av CW2 — 3 B4
Derwent Cl CW5 — 13 G3
Deva Rd CW2 — 6 A5
Dewes St CW1 — 7 E5
Dickens Cl CW11 — 4 A3
Dig La CW2 — 14 A3
Dillors Cft CW1 — 6 D1
Dingle Bank CW11 — 5 E2
Dingle La CW11 — 5 E3
Doddington Dr CW11 — 5 F1
Doddington Rd CW2 — 10 D1
Dog La CW5 — 12 C3
Dorfold Cl CW11 — 5 F2
Dorfold Dr CW5 — 12 B4
Dorfold St CW1 — 3 B3
Dorric Way CW1 — 7 E3
Dove Cl CW11 — 4 D1
Dovecote Cl CW2 — 11 E4
Drayton Cres CW1 — 7 H5
Drovers Way CW11 — 4 D4
Drury Cl CW1 — 8 A5
Dryden Cl CW2 — 10 D3
Duchy Rd CW1 — 16 A4
Duke St CW2 — 3 A3
Dukes Cres CW1 — 4 D1
Dunham Cl CW11 — 5 F3
Dunham Cres CW2 — 11 E4
Dunnillow Fld CW5 — 13 E5
Dunstone Cl CW2 — 10 D2
Dunwoody Way CW1,2 — 3 A2
Dutton Way,
Crewe CW1 — 7 E4

Dutton Way,
Nantwich CW5 — 12 C5

Eadie Gro CW1 — 6 D3
Eardley Pl CW1 — 7 E5
Earle St CW1 — 3 C2
Earls Rd CW2 — 14 B2
East Av CW2 — 15 H2
Eastern Rd CW5 — 13 H3
Eaton Cl CW11 — 5 E2
Eaton St CW2 — 3 B3
Edgewood Dr CW2 — 10 D5
Edinburgh Dr CW2 — 10 B5
Edleston Rd CW2 — 3 B3
Edmund Wright Way
CW5 — 12 A3
Edward Ho*,
Princes Ct CW2 — 10 C1
Edward St CW2 — 3 C6
Edwards Av CW2 — 14 B1
Edwards Cl CW2 — 14 B2
Elanor Rd CW11 — 4 A2
Eleanor Cl CW1 — 6 C5
Electra Ho CW1 — 16 B2
Electra Way CW1 — 16 A1
Electricity St CW2 — 3 B4
Eliot Cl CW1 — 8 A5
Elizabeth Cl CW11 — 4 A2
Elizabeth St CW1 — 7 E5
Ellesmere Cl CW11 — 4 C1
Ellis St CW1 — 7 E4
Ellwood Gro CW2 — 15 E3
Elm Cl, Crewe CW2 — 10 B2
Elm Cl, Nantwich CW5 — 12 C4
Elm Dr CW1 — 7 G4
Elm Ho*,
Brook Cl CW11 — 5 E3
Elm Tree La CW1 — 4 A1
Elmstead Cres CW1 — 6 C2
Elton Crossings Rd
CW11 — 4 A2
Elton La CW11 — 9 E1
Elton Rd CW11 — 4 A4
Elwood Way CW5 — 13 E5
Elworth Rd CW11 — 4 A3
Elworth St CW11 — 4 D2
Emerald Dr CW11 — 5 F1
Empress Dr CW2 — 11 E1
Enfield Cl CW2 — 14 B3
Englefield Cl CW1 — 6 D2
Ennerdale Rd CW2 — 10 A1
Eric Dr CW1 — 4 A2
Ernest St CW2 — 11 F2
Ernley Cl CW5 — 12 B3
Etherow Cl CW1 — 4 B2
Ettiley Av CW11 — 4 A4
Europa Ho CW1 — 16 A2
Eva St CW11 — 4 A1
Evans St CW1 — 7 E4

Fairbrook CW2 — 10 B2
Fairburn Av CW2 — 6 C6
Fairfax Dr CW5 — 12 B3
Fairfield Av CW11 — 4 D4
Fairview Av CW2 — 15 G2
Falcon Dr CW1 — 7 E2
Fallowfield Ct CW1 — 6 D4
Falmouth Rd CW2 — 6 D4
Fanshawe Walk CW2 — 11 F4
Farmer Cl CW2 — 6 C6
Farmleigh Dr CW1 — 6 C2
Farndale Cl CW2 — 10 D6
Fern Ct CW1 — 11 H1
Fernbank Cl CW1 — 8 A6
Ferndale Cl,
Crewe CW2 — 15 G1
Ferndale Cl,
Sandbach CW11 — 5 F4
Field Av CW2 — 10 C3
Field La CW2 — 10 A2
Field Vw CW1 — 8 A5
Fields Dr CW1 — 4 D3
Fields Rd CW1 — 8 D6
Fields View Cl CW5 — 14 B6
Firbeck Gdns CW2 — 6 A6
First Av, Crewe CW1 — 11 H2
First Av,
Sandbach CW11 — 4 D4
First Wood St CW5 — 12 B3
Firwood Walk CW2 — 11 F4
Fishermans Cl CW11 — 9 F3
Flag La CW1,2 — 3 A4
Flat La CW11 — 5 E3
Fletcher St CW1 — 7 E5
Flixton Dr CW2 — 10 D2
Flour Mill Way CW1 — 16 A1

Flowers Cft CW5 — 13 E4
Flowers La CW1 — 6 B1
Ford Cl CW5 — 7 E5
Ford La CW1 — 7 E5
Forge Flds CW11 — 4 C6
Forge St CW1 — 3 C3
Foulkes Av CW1 — 6 C4
Foundry La CW11 — 4 A2
Four Seasons Cl CW2 — 11 E4
Fourth Av CW1 — 16 A3
Fourways CW2 — 15 G1
Fox Covert Way CW1 — 6 D1
Foxes Hollow CW1 — 7 H3
Foxglove Cl CW2 — 11 E5
Frances St CW2 — 3 B6
Frank Bott Av CW1 — 6 D3
Frank Webb Av CW1 — 6 D3
Franklyn Av CW2 — 11 E1
Frederick Ho*,
Princes Ct CW2 — 10 C1
Freshfields CW2 — 10 C5
Front Cl CW11 — 5 E3
Fulbeck Cl CW2 — 10 D3
Fuller Dr CW2 — 10 D4
Furber St CW1 — 7 F5
Furnival St CW2 — 3 A6

Gainsborough Rd CW2 — 3 A4
Galway Gro CW2 — 14 B3
Game St CW11 — 4 D6
Garnett Cl CW5 — 12 D5
Gatefield St CW1 — 3 A2
Gateway CW1 — 11 H2
Gawsworth Av CW2 — 10 C1
Gawsworth Dr CW11 — 5 F1
Gawsworth Ho CW1 — 16 A2
George Ho*,
Princes Ct CW2 — 10 C1
George St CW11 — 4 B1
Georges Walk CW1 — 5 E3
Gerard Dr CW5 — 12 A5
Gibson Cl CW1 — 12 A3
Gibson Cres CW11 — 4 A3
Gillow Cl CW1 — 6 D2
Gingerbread La CW5 — 13 H4
Gladstone St CW5 — 13 H3
Glaisdale Cl CW2 — 10 D6
Glamis Cl CW2 — 10 B4
Glebe Cl CW5 — 14 A6
Glover St CW1 — 6 D5
Goddard Ct*,
Cornwall Gro CW1 — 7 E5
Goddard St CW1 — 6 D5
Godwin Cres CW2 — 14 B2
Goldsmith Dr CW11 — 4 A3
Goodalls Cnr CW2 — 14 C3
Gorsey Bank Cres CW5 — 14 A6
Goulden St CW1 — 6 D5
Gowy Cl CW11 — 4 B1
Grace Cl CW1 — 8 D6
Grafton Cl CW1 — 8 C5
Grand Junction
Retail Pk CW1 — 3 D3
Grand Junction Way
CW1 — 3 D3
Grange Cl, Crewe CW1 — 11 H1
Grange Cl,
Sandbach CW11 — 4 C2
Grange Way CW11 — 4 B1
Grasmere Av CW2 — 6 B5
Green La CW5 — 13 H4
Green St CW11 — 5 E2
Greenacres, Crewe CW1 — 7 F4
Greenacres,
Sandbach CW11 — 4 D2
Greenbank Cl CW5 — 13 G3
Greendale Gdns CW1 — 7 H4
Greenfields Av CW2 — 14 B3
Greenway CW1 — 7 F3
Grenville Cl CW1 — 7 H4
Gresty Green Rd CW2 — 11 F4
Gresty La CW2 — 10 D6
Gresty Rd CW2 — 3 D6
Gresty Ter CW1 — 7 H6
Greystone Pk CW1 — 3 D1
Green Ct CW5 — 12 C3
Groby Rd CW1 — 7 G1
Grocotts Row CW5 — 12 C4
Grosvenor St CW1 — 7 E5
Guillemot Cl CW1 — 8 A5
Guttercroft CW1 — 8 D4

Haddon Cl CW2 — 10 D5
Hadyn Jones Dr CW5 — 12 D5
Hall Dr CW5 — 13 G3
Hall O'Shaw St CW1 — 3 D2
Hallams Dr CW5 — 13 E5

Hallshaw Av CW1 — 7 H5
Halton Dr CW2 — 6 A5
Hamilton Cl CW1 — 8 C5
Hammond St CW2 — 3 A4
Hanbury Cl CW2 — 11 E4
Handforth Rd CW2 — 10 B1
Harding Rd CW5 — 12 A4
Hardwicke Ct CW1 — 7 H6
Hardy Cl CW2 — 10 C4
Hargrave Av CW2 — 10 C1
Harris Cl CW1 — 7 E1
Harrow Cl CW2 — 10 D3
Hartford Cl CW11 — 5 F2
Harvey Av CW5 — 12 D3
Haslemere Way CW1 — 7 F4
Haslington By-Pass,
Crewe CW1 — 8 B6
Haslington By-Pass,
Sandbach CW11 — 9 E2
Hassall Rd,
Sandbach CW11 — 5 F6
Hassall Rd,
Wheelock Heath CW11 — 9 F2
Hatchmere Cl CW11 — 4 C2
Haweswater Av CW1 — 7 E1
Hawk St CW1 — 5 E3
Hawksey Dr CW5 — 12 D4
Hawthorn Av CW5 — 12 D4
Hawthorn Gro CW1 — 7 G3
Hawthorn La CW2 — 10 C2
Hawthorne Dr CW11 — 5 F3
Hayes Cl CW5 — 12 C2
Hayling Cl CW1 — 7 E2
Haymoor Green Rd
CW5 — 13 H6
Hazel Gro CW1 — 7 F3
Healey Cl CW1 — 6 D2
Heath Av CW11 — 5 G3
Heath Cl CW11 — 5 G3
Heath Rd CW11 — 5 F3
Heath St CW1 — 3 B1
Heath Vw,
Haslington CW1 — 8 D6
Heath Vw,
Weston CW2 — 15 H1
Heathgate Pl CW2 — 10 D4
Heathfield Av CW1 — 3 A1
Heathfield Cl CW5 — 12 D3
Heathside CW5 — 12 D3
Heaward Cl CW2 — 14 B2
Hellath Wen CW5 — 12 C6
Helmsdale Cl CW1 — 7 E4
Hendon Cl CW1 — 8 A4
Henry St, Crewe CW1 — 7 G5
Henry St,
Haslington CW1 — 8 D5
Henshall Dr CW11 — 5 F1
Herald Pk CW1 — 3 D5
Herbert St CW1 — 8 A4
Herbert Swindells Cl
CW2 — 11 F3
Herdman St CW2 — 3 C5
Heron Cres CW1 — 8 A5
Herrick Cl CW2 — 10 C4
Hesketh Cft CW1 — 6 D2
Hewitt St CW2 — 3 C6
Heywood Grn CW2 — 11 F4
Hidcote Cl CW2 — 10 D4
High St, Crewe CW2 — 3 B3
High St, Nantwich CW5 — 12 B3
High St,
Sandbach CW11 — 5 E3
Highfield Dr CW5 — 12 D2
Highgate Cl CW1 — 6 D2
Hightown, Crewe CW1 — 3 A1
Hightown,
Sandbach CW11 — 5 E3
Hill St, Crewe CW1 — 3 C2
Hill St, Sandbach CW11 — 4 A2
Hillfield Gdns CW5 — 12 C5
Hillfield Pl CW5 — 12 C4
Hillside Cl CW2 — 12 C4
Hillside Dr CW1 — 7 H5
Hind Heath La CW1 — 4 C5
Hind Heath Rd CW11 — 4 B4
Hinde St CW5 — 12 A4
Hinton Rd CW2 — 11 F4
Hirsch Cl CW5 — 13 E4
Hobbs Cl CW1 — 8 D6
Hodgkin Cl CW5 — 12 D5
Holbury Cl CW1 — 7 E1
Holland Cl CW11 — 5 F4
Holland St CW1 — 7 E3
Holly Heath Cl CW11 — 5 F4
Holly Mt CW2 — 15 E2
Hollybush Cres CW5 — 13 H3
Hollyfields CW11 — 9 F1

Holmlea Dr CW1 — 11 H1
Holmshaw La CW1 — 9 E4
Holt St CW1 — 7 E6
Holyrood Dr CW2 — 10 B4
Hope St, Crewe CW2 — 3 C6
Hope St,
Sandbach CW11 — 5 E3
Hornby Dr CW5 — 12 D3
Horton Way CW5 — 12 D4
Hospital St,
Crewe CW1 — 7 G4
Hospital St,
Nantwich CW5 — 12 C4
Hothershall Cl CW1 — 7 E1
Houndings La,
Cold Moss Heath CW11 — 5 E4
Houndings La,
Sandbach CW11 — 4 D5
Hove Cl CW1 — 7 E2
Howard St CW1 — 8 A4
Howbeck Cres CW5 — 14 A6
Howbeck Walk CW1 — 11 F4
Howth Way CW1 — 16 A2
Hughes Dr CW2 — 6 C6
Hulme St CW1 — 6 C5
Hungerford Av CW1 — 7 H6
Hungerford Cl CW11 — 4 D4
Hungerford Pl CW11 — 4 D4
Hungerford Rd CW1 — 7 H6
Hungerford Ter CW1 — 8 A6
Hunter Av CW2 — 11 F5
Huntersfield CW2 — 14 A3
Hurn Cl CW1 — 7 E2
Hythe Av CW1 — 7 E1

Imperial Mews CW2 — 3 C4

Jack La CW2 — 16 D4
Jackson Av CW5 — 12 D4
Jackson St CW1 — 6 D4
James Atkinson Way
CW1 — 6 C3
James Hall St CW5 — 12 C4
Jan Palach Av CW5 — 12 C5
Jesmond Cres CW2 — 11 E2
Jessop Way CW1 — 8 D6
John Gresty Dr CW5 — 13 H3
John St CW1 — 3 A1
Jubilee Av CW1 — 11 E1
Jubilee Gdns CW5 — 12 C5
Jubilee Ter CW5 — 12 C4

Keats Dr CW2 — 10 D4
Kemble Cl CW2 — 11 E4
Kempton Av CW1 — 7 E3
Kenilworth Cl CW2 — 10 D5
Kensington Dr CW5 — 13 H4
Kents Green La CW1 — 9 E3
Kents La CW1 — 7 F1
Kestrel Dr CW1 — 6 D2
Keswick Cl CW2 — 10 B1
Kettell Av CW1 — 6 C4
Kidston Dr CW1 — 6 C3
Kiln La CW5 — 14 B6
Kinder Dr CW2 — 10 A1
King Dr CW11 — 4 D2
King Pl CW5 — 12 C3
King St, Crewe CW1 — 3 D2
King St,
Sandbach CW11 — 4 B1
Kingfisher Cl CW1 — 12 C1
Kings Ct CW5 — 12 B3
Kings Dr CW5 — 10 B4
Kings La CW5 — 12 A3
Kings Mdw CW2 — 15 E4
Kingsley Ct*,
Station Rd CW11 — 4 A1
Kingsley Rd CW1 — 8 C5
Kingsway CW2 — 11 E1
Kinloch Cl CW1 — 7 E4
Kipling Way CW1 — 8 A5
Knights Way CW2 — 14 A3

Laburnum Av,
Crewe CW2 — 10 B2
Laburnum Av,
Nantwich CW5 — 12 D4
Laburnum Gro CW1 — 7 G4
Lady Helen Walk CW5 — 12 C3
Laidon Av CW2 — 10 D4
Lakeside Vw CW5 — 12 B6
Lambert Cres CW5 — 12 A3
Lambourn Dr CW1 — 6 D1
Lancaster Flds CW1 — 16 A2
Langdale Rd CW2 — 10 A1
Langley Cl CW5 — 5 F1
Langley Dr CW2 — 10 D2
Lansdowne Rd CW1 — 7 H5

18

Lanyard Way CW11 5 F6
Larch Av CW2 15 E1
Larch Rd CW2 10 B2
Larkspur Cl CW5 12 C1
Latham Rd CW11 4 D4
Latimer Dr CW2 6 D6
Laura St CW2 11 G3
Laurel Cl CW11 5 E4
Laurel Dr CW2 10 C2
Laureston Av CW1 8 A5
Lawford Cl CW1 6 C2
Lawrence Cl CW11 4 A3
Lawrence St CW1 3 B2
Lawton St CW2 3 B4
Lawton Way CW11 4 B1
Lea Av CW1 7 H6
Lea Cl CW11 5 F4
Lea Dr CW5 12 A4
Lear Dr CW2 10 C4
Ledbury Dr CW2 10 D5
Leighton Vw CW1 6 D3
Lewis Cl CW5 13 E4
Lewis St CW2 3 A3
Leyland Gro CW1 8 D6
Lightley Cl CW11 4 D5
Lime Cl CW11 4 D2
Lime Gro CW2 14 C2
Lime St CW1 7 F3
Lime Tree Av CW1 7 G3
Limes Cl CW1 8 C5
Linden Ct, Sandbach CW11 4 C6
Linden Ct, Crewe CW1 11 H1
Linden Dr CW1 7 H6
Lingfield Dr CW1 7 E3
Linnet Cl CW1 6 C3
Lochleven Rd CW2 10 D5
Lockitt St CW2 3 C4
Lodge Rd CW11 4 B3
Lodgefields Dr CW2 6 A6
Lomax Rd CW5 13 G3
London Rd, Nantwich CW5 12 D4
London Rd, Sandbach CW11 4 A1
Lord St CW2 3 C4
Lords Mill Rd CW2 14 B3
Love La CW5 12 B4
Ludford St CW1 7 F5
Ludlow Av CW1 11 H1
Lunt Av CW2 3 A6
Lyceum Cl CW1 6 D2
Lyceum Way CW1 6 D2
Lydgate Cl CW2 10 C4
Lynbrook Rd CW1 7 H6
Lyncroft Cl CW1 8 A6
Lynton Gro CW1 8 D4
Lynton Way CW2 10 D4
Lyon St CW1 3 C2

Mablins La CW1 7 E1
Macon Ct CW1 11 G1
Macon Way CW1 11 H2
Madeley St CW2 11 F3
Magdalen Ct CW2 10 D3
Main Rd, Shavington CW2 14 A3
Main Rd, Wybunbury CW5 14 A5
Main Rd, Weston CW2 16 C5
Mainwaring Cl CW5 13 E5
Maisterson Ct CW5 12 C3
Malbank CW5 12 B3
Malbank Rd CW2 6 A6
Mallard Way CW1 16 B2
Malory Cl CW1 8 A4
Malvern Cl CW2 14 B3
Manifold Cl CW11 4 B1
Manning St CW2 11 G3
Manor Av CW2 10 D3
Manor Ct CW2 11 E3
Manor Rd, Nantwich CW5 12 B2
Manor Rd, Sandbach CW11 5 F3
Manor Rd North CW5 12 B1
Manor Way, Crewe CW2 11 E3
Manor Way, Sandbach CW11 5 G3
Mansion Ct CW5 12 C4
Maple Cl CW11 5 F3
Maple Gro CW1 7 G3
March St CW1 3 D1
Mark St CW5 13 H2
Market Centre CW2 3 B1
Market Cl CW1 7 F5
Market Sq, Crewe CW1 3 B2
Market Sq, Sandbach CW11 5 E3
Market St, Crewe CW1,2 3 B3
Market St, Meredith St CW1 7 F5
Market St, Nantwich CW5 12 C3
Marlborough Cl CW2 10 B4
Marlborough Dr CW11 5 E1
Marley Av CW1 7 E3
Marlowe Cl, Crewe CW2 10 C4
Marlowe Cl, Sandbach CW11 4 A4
Marlowe Dr CW5 12 C5
Marple Cres CW2 10 B2
Marriott Rd CW11 4 C6
Marsh Green Rd CW11 4 A1
Marsh La CW5 12 A5
Marshfield Av CW2 6 A5
Marshfield Bank CW2 6 A6
Marton Cl CW2 15 E3
Martree Ct CW11 4 B1
Mary St CW1 3 D1
Marys Gate CW2 10 B4
Masefield Dr CW1 7 H6
Masefield Way CW11 4 A4
Massey Cl CW5 13 E5
Mavor Ct CW1 7 E6
Maw Green Cl CW1 7 H3
Maw Green Rd CW1 7 H3
Maw La CW1 8 A3
Maxwell St CW2 3 B5
Mayfield Mews CW1 6 C4
Mayflower Rd CW5 12 C5
McLaren St CW1 7 E3
McNeill Av CW1 6 C5
Meadow Av CW2 15 H1
Meadow Cl CW2 14 D1
Meadow Dr CW2 10 C5
Meadowgate Cl CW11 4 A4
Meadowvale Cl CW5 12 C1
Meeanee Dr CW5 12 A4
Melbourne Gro CW1 8 C5
Melford Cl CW2 11 E4
Mellor St CW1 7 G5
Melrose Dr CW1 6 D2
Mercer Way CW5 12 C1
Merchants Ct CW1 7 F3
Mercian Cl CW2 14 B2
Mercury Ho CW1 3 D5
Mere Cl CW1 8 D5
Mere Ct CW2 15 H1
Mere Rd CW2 15 G1
Mere St CW1 8 D5
Merebank Rd CW2 11 E3
Merebrook Walk CW2 11 F4
Meredith St CW1 7 F5
Merlin Way CW1 6 D2
Merrills Av CW2 6 B5
Merrivale Rd CW2 10 D4
Meynell Cl CW2 10 C4
Mickle Wright Av CW1 7 G4
Middlewich Rd, Crewe CW1,2 6 A1
Middlewich Rd, Nantwich CW5 12 C2
Middlewich Rd, Sandbach CW11 4 B2
Middlewich St CW1 7 F3
Mika Cl CW5 12 A3
Mill Bridge Cl CW1 8 A6
Mill Hill Dr CW11 4 D4
Mill Hill La CW11 4 D4
Mill La CW11 4 D6
Mill Row CW11 5 F3
Mill St, Crewe CW2 3 C4
Mill St, Nantwich CW5 12 B4
Mill Way CW5 12 D6
Millbeck Cl CW2 15 H1
Millbuck Way CW11 4 A3
Millcroft CW11 9 F1
Millenium Gate CW1 16 A2
Millfields CW5 12 A4
Millrace Dr CW2 11 E4
Mills Way CW1 7 E1
Millstone La CW5 12 C4
Milne Cl CW2 10 C3
Milton Dr CW2 10 C4
Milton Way CW11 4 A3
Minshull New Rd CW1 6 C2
Mirion St CW1 3 D2
Monck Dr CW5 12 B2
Monk St CW1 6 D5
Monks La, Crewe CW1 6 C4
Monks La, Nantwich CW5 12 C3
Monks Orch CW5 12 C3
Montrose Cl CW2 14 A3
Moorfields CW5 13 H3
Moorlands Dr CW5 14 A6
Moreton Cl CW11 5 F2
Moreton Rd CW2 10 C1
Morgan Cl CW2 6 C6
Morgan Walk CW5 12 B2
Mornington Cl CW11 4 A2
Mortimer Dr CW11 5 F4
Moss Cft CW1 6 D2
Moss Dale Cl CW2 6 B6
Moss La, Crewe CW1 6 C2
Moss La, Nantwich CW5 14 A5
Moss La, Sandbach CW11 4 A1
Moss Lane Bsns Centre CW11 4 A2
Mossfields CW1 6 D1
Mossford Av CW1 7 E3
Moston Rd CW11 4 A4
Mottram Dr CW5 12 D4
Mount Cl CW5 12 D3
Mount Dr CW5 12 D3
Mount Pleasant, Crewe CW1 7 E4
Mount Pleasant, Haslington CW1 9 E6
Mountbatten Ct CW2 10 D1
Mulberry Gdns CW11 4 A1
Mulberry Rd CW2 10 B2
Mulcaster Ct CW1 8 D5
Murrayfield Dr CW5 13 G3
Myrtle St CW2 3 B4
Mytton Dr CW5 12 A3

Nantwich By-Pass CW5 12 B1
Nantwich Rd CW2 3 B6
Narrow La CW1 8 B6
Naylor Cres CW5 12 D5
Nelson St CW2 3 B5
Nesfield Ct CW11 9 F2
Nesfield Dr CW11 9 F3
Nessina Gro CW2 10 C4
Neville St CW2 11 F3
Nevis Dr CW2 10 A1
New Cl CW1 6 D1
New St, Crewe CW1 8 D5
New St, Sandbach CW11 4 A1
Newall Av CW11 4 D3
Newbold Way CW5 12 B5
Newbury Av CW1 7 E3
Newcastle Rd, Blakelow CW5 13 G5
Newcastle Rd, Crewe CW2 15 E4
Newcastle Rd, Sandbach CW11 5 H4
Newcastle Rd, Shavington CW2 14 A3
Newcastle Rd, Willaston CW5 13 G4
Newcastle St CW1 6 D5
Newdigate St CW1 3 B1
Newfield Dr CW1 7 G5
Newfield St CW11 5 E2
Newland Way CW5 13 E5
Newton St CW1 7 F5
Newtons Cres CW11 9 F2
Newtons Gro CW11 9 E3
Newtons La CW11 9 E3
Nicholas Ct CW5 12 C4
Nigel Gresley Cl CW1 8 A6
Nile St CW2 3 A6
Nixon St CW1 6 C5
Nixons Row CW5 12 A3
Norbreck Av CW2 11 E2
North Cfts CW5 12 C3
North St CW1 7 F3
North Stafford St CW1 3 C2
North Way CW2 14 D1
Northfield Pl CW2 14 B1
Norton Way CW11 4 A2
Nursery Cl, Crewe CW2 10 C2
Nursery Cl, Hough CW2 15 E4
Nursery Cl, Shavington CW2 14 B3
Nutfield Av CW1 7 E3
Nuthurst Gdns CW5 12 C4

Oak Bank Cl CW5 13 H4
Oak Ho*, Brook Ct CW11 5 E3
Oak St, Crewe CW2 3 B3
Oak St, Sandbach CW11 4 A1
Oak Tree Cl CW1 7 H5
Oak Tree Dr CW1 7 H5
Oakhurst Dr CW2 11 E5
Oakland Av CW1 8 C5
Oakley Cl CW11 4 D1
Oakley St CW1 7 F5
Oakmere Cl CW11 4 C1
Oakwood Cres, Crewe CW2 6 B6
Oakwood Cres, Sandbach CW11 5 G3
Oat Mkt CW5 12 B3
Offley Av CW11 5 E2
Offley Rd CW11 5 E2
Old Gorse Cl CW2 10 B1
Old Hall Gdns*, High St CW11 5 E3
Old Mill Rd CW11 5 E3
Old Park Rd CW1 16 D5
Oldfield Rd CW11 4 C5
Orchard Cres CW5 12 C6
Orchard Ct CW1 8 D5
Orchard St, Crewe CW1 3 A1
Orchard St, Nantwich CW5 13 H3
Ordsall Cl CW11 4 C6
Ormerod Cl CW11 5 E3
Osborne Cl CW11 4 A4
Osborne Gro CW2 14 B2
Ossmere Cl CW11 4 C1
Owen St CW2 3 A6
Oxford St CW1 6 D5

Padmore Cl CW1 6 C3
Padstow Cl CW1 7 E2
Padworth Pl CW1 7 E1
Page Gro CW2 14 B3
Pall Mall CW5 12 C4
Palmerston Cl CW1 8 C5
Park Dr CW2 10 B3
Park Est CW2 14 D1
Park Fld CW1 6 D1
Park House Dr CW11 5 F1
Park La CW11 4 C3
Park Rd, Crewe CW1 8 D5
Park Rd, Nantwich CW5 12 B5
Park Rd, Willaston CW5 13 F3
Park Vw CW5 12 C3
Parkers Rd CW1 6 D1
Parkfield Dr CW5 12 C5
Parkmills Cl CW5 13 H3
Parkstone Dr CW1 7 E1
Pear Tree Av CW1 7 E3
Pear Tree Cl CW11 5 H3
Pear Tree Fld CW5 13 E5
Peckforton Cl CW11 4 B1
Pedley St CW2 3 C6
Peel Sq CW1 7 E5
Peel St CW1 7 E5
Pelham Cl CW1 8 D4
Pelican Cl CW1 8 A5
Penbrook Cl CW2 10 A1
Penda Way CW11 5 E3
Pendle Cl CW1 8 A4
Penlington Ct CW5 12 D3
Pepper St CW5 12 B3
Peter Destapleigh Way CW5 12 D6
Peter Ellson Cl CW2 11 F3
Peter Pl CW1 7 E5
Petworth Cl CW2 11 E4
Pickering Way CW5 12 D5
Pickmere Cl CW11 4 C2
Pickwick Cl CW11 5 F1
Pillory St CW5 12 B4
Pine Gro CW11 5 F3
Pine Walk CW5 12 C5
Pinewood Ct CW2 11 E5
Pinfold Cl CW5 14 A6
Pit La CW2 14 D4
Plane Tree Dr CW1 7 G4
Plant St CW11 4 D2
Platt Av CW11 4 D2
Pollard Dr CW5 13 E4
Pool La CW11 9 F3
Pool Meadows Rd CW1 8 C5
Pool Vw CW11 9 F3
Poplar Gro CW1 7 H5
Portland Gro CW1 8 D4
Potter Cl CW5 13 H4
Pratchitts Row CW5 12 C4
Preece Ct CW1 7 E5
Price Av CW11 4 D4
Price Dr CW11 4 D4
Primrose Av CW1 8 C5
Primrose Hill CW2 6 B5
Prince Albert St CW1 3 C3
Prince Edward St CW5 12 B2
Princes Ct CW2 10 C1
Princess Cl CW2 10 C4
Princess Dr, Crewe CW2 10 B4
Princess Dr, Nantwich CW5 12 D3
Princess Dr, Sandbach CW11 4 D1
Princess Gro CW2 10 C4
Princess St CW1 7 E4
Prior Cl CW2 10 C3
Priory Cl CW1 6 D2
Priscilla St CW1 7 G6
Probert Cl CW2 6 C6
Proctors La CW11 4 A4
Prunus Rd CW1 7 G4
Pyms La CW1 6 A4
Pyrus Av CW1 7 G4

Quakers Coppice CW1 16 A3
Queen St CW1 3 D2
Queens Dr, Nantwich CW5 12 A5
Queens Dr, Sandbach CW11 4 D1
Queens Park Dr CW2 6 C6
Queens Park Gdns CW2 6 B6
Queensway CW1 3 B2

Radbroke Cl CW11 5 F1
Radcliffe Rd CW11 4 C6
Radnor Cl CW11 4 B2
Railbrook Ct CW2 3 D5
Railton Av CW1 6 D3
Railway St CW2 3 C6
Rainbow St CW1 3 D2
Ramsbottom St CW1 7 E6
Randle Bennett Cl CW11 4 B2
Raven Cl CW11 4 D1
Ravenscroft Cl CW11 5 F2
Ravenscroft Rd CW2 10 B1
Ray Av CW5 12 D1
Readesdale Av CW2 10 C2
Rectory Cl, Crewe CW2 10 B4
Rectory Cl, Nantwich CW5 12 C3
Red Lion La CW5 12 B3
Redesmere Cl CW11 4 C2
Regent Cl CW2 14 B3
Regents Gate CW5 13 E4
Reid St CW1 7 E4
Remer St CW1 7 G3
Renaissance Way CW1 8 A6
Repton Dr CW1 8 D4
Reynolds La CW11 5 H2
Rhoden St CW1 8 A4
Rhodes Cl CW1 8 D6
Richard Moon St CW1 3 A2
Richard St CW1 7 E6
Richardson Cl, Crewe CW2 14 C1
Richardson Cl, Sandbach CW11 4 A3
Richmond Cl CW11 4 B2
Richmond Rd CW1 7 H5
Ridgway St CW1 7 G5
Ridley Cl CW2 15 E4
Rigby Av CW1 6 D3
Rigbys Row CW5 12 C4
Rigg St CW1 7 E5
Riley Cl CW11 4 B4
Rimsdale Cl CW2 10 D5
Ripon Dr CW2 10 D5
Riverbank Cl CW5 12 C1
Riverside CW5 12 B4
Road One CW1 16 D4
Road Two CW1 16 D4
Robin Cl CW11 4 D1
Rochester Cres CW1 7 H5
Rockwood Av CW2 10 D1
Rockwood Cl CW2 10 D1
Roedean Walk CW1 7 F4
Rolls Av CW1 6 C3
Roman Way CW11 4 B2
Rook St CW2 3 A5
Rookery Cl, Nantwich CW5 12 C4
Rookery Cl, Sandbach CW11 4 A4
Rookery Dr CW5 12 C5
Rope Bank Av CW2 10 D5
Rope La CW2 10 C5

Rose Ter CW1	7 E5	Shrewbridge Cres CW5	12 B4
Roseberry Way CW1	8 C5	Shrewbridge Rd CW5	12 B5
Rosehill Rd CW2	10 D3	Siddals Ct*,	
Rosewood Cl CW1	7 H4	Taylor Dr CW5	12 A3
Rostherne Way CW11	4 C2	Sidings Vw CW2	3 C4
Rowan Cl CW11	4 C2	Silver Ter CW11	5 G3
Rowton Rd CW2	6 A6	Simpson Ct CW1	6 D1
Royce Cl CW1	6 D3	Singleton Av CW1	7 F4
Rudheath Cl CW2	6 A5	Skeath Cl CW11	5 G3
Rufford Cl CW2	10 D4	Skylark Cl CW1	6 C3
Ruscoe Av CW11	4 B3	Smallbrook Walk CW4	11 F4
Rushton Dr CW2	15 E4	Smallman Rd CW2	11 E3
Ruskin Rd CW2	3 A4	Smith Gro CW1	6 C4
Russell Dr CW1	8 C5	Smithfield La CW11	5 F3
Rydal Mt CW1	7 E1	Smithy La CW1	6 B2
Ryde Cl CW1	7 E2	Smithy Walk CW11	4 C6
Ryebank Av CW1	7 E3	Snape Rd CW2	11 F4
		Snowdon Dr CW2	10 A1
St Albans Dr CW5	12 C5	Somerford Av CW2	10 D1
Saint Andrews Av CW2	11 F3	Somerford Cl CW11	5 F1
Saint Andrews Ct CW2	11 F3	Somerley Cl CW1	7 E2
Saint Annes La CW5	12 B3	Somerville St CW2	11 E2
Saint Clairs St CW2	11 G3	Sorbus Dr CW1	7 G4
Saint Johns Way CW1	5 G3	South Av CW1	8 D6
Saint Josephs Way		South Cfts CW2	12 C3
CW5	12 D4	South St CW2	3 C6
Saint Lawrence Ct CW5	12 C3	Southbank Av CW2	14 C2
Saint Marys Rd CW5	12 C2	Southey Cl CW11	4 A3
Saint Marys St CW1	3 A2	Southfields Cl CW5	14 A6
Saint Matthews Cl CW1	8 D5	Southmere Ct CW11	16 A2
Saint Michaels Vw CW1	7 E5	Spencer Cl CW1	10 D4
Saint Pauls Cl CW1	3 A1	Spinney Dr CW2	15 G1
Saint Pauls St CW1	3 A1	Spring Gdns,	
Saint Peters Rise CW11	4 B2	Crewe CW1	7 G5
Saint Stephens Ct CW11	4 A2	Spring Gdns,	
Salander Cres CW2	10 D5	Nantwich CW5	12 C4
Salisbury Av CW2	11 E3	Springfield Dr CW2	10 C5
Salisbury Cl CW2	11 E3	**Springvale Bsns Centre**	
Salt Line Way CW11	4 A2	**CW11**	**4 A3**
Saltmeadows CW5	12 A3	Springwell Cl CW2	11 E4
Samuel St CW1	3 A1	Stafford St CW1	7 E5
Sanbec Way*,		Stalbridge Rd CW2	3 A5
Penda Way CW11	5 E3	Stamford Av CW2	3 A4
Sanderson Cl CW2	11 F4	Stamp Av CW1	7 F4
Sandford Rd CW5	12 D2	Stanier Cl CW1	8 A6
Sandhurst Av CW2	10 D3	Stanley St CW1	3 A2
Sandiway Rd CW1	6 D4	Stannerhouse La CW11	5 G6
Sandon Park Gdns CW2	6 A6	Stanope Av CW1	11 H1
Sandon St CW1	3 C3	Stanthorne Av CW2	10 C1
Sandown Rd CW1	7 F3	Stanyer Ct CW5	12 D5
Sandringham Dr CW2	10 B4	Stapeley Ter CW5	12 D4
Sandy La,		Station Rd,	
Elworth CW11	4 A4	Nantwich CW5	12 C4
Sandy La,		Station Rd,	
Heath CW11	9 G2	Sandbach CW11	4 A1
Sandylands Pk CW2	10 A5	Station Vw,	
Savoy Rd CW1	16 A4	Nantwich CW5	12 C4
Saxon Pl CW11	4 D3	Station Vw,	
Scaife Rd CW5	12 C3	Sandbach CW11	4 A1
School Cres CW1	7 H6	Stephenson Dr CW1	8 A6
School La,		Sterne Cl CW11	4 A3
Elworth CW11	4 A2	Stewart St CW2	10 D1
School La,		Stock La CW5	14 A5
Nantwich CW5	12 C3	Stonebridge Rd CW5	12 B6
School La,		Stoneley Av CW1	7 F2
Sandbach CW11	5 H3	Stoneley Rd CW1	7 F3
School St CW1	8 D5	Strathaven Av CW2	10 B4
Scott Av CW1	4 A3	Stringer Av CW11	5 F3
Scott Cl CW11	4 A3	Sunart Cl CW2	10 D6
Seagull Cl CW1	8 A5	Sundale Dr CW2	10 A1
Seaton Cl CW1	7 E2	Sunnybank Rd CW2	6 B5
Second Av, Crewe CW1	11 H3	Sunnymill Dr CW1	4 D3
Second Av,		Surrey St CW1	7 G6
Sandbach CW11	4 D4	Sutton Cl CW5	12 A3
Second Wood St CW5	12 B3	Swallow Dr CW1	4 D1
Sedgemere Av CW1	6 D2	Swallowfield Cl CW2	10 D4
Selsey Cl CW1	7 E2	Sweet Briar Cres CW2	10 C1
Selworthy Dr CW1	6 D3	Sweettooth La CW11	4 D2
Shakespeare Dr CW1	8 A5	Swettenham Cl CW11	5 F2
Shannon Cl CW5	13 G3	Swift Cl CW2	10 C4
Sharnbrook Dr CW2	6 B6	Swinburne Dr CW1	8 A5
Shelburne Dr CW1	8 C5	Swine Mkt CW5	12 B3
Shelley Ct CW11	4 A3	Swinnerton St CW2	11 F2
Shelley Dr CW2	10 C3	Sycamore Av CW1	7 G3
Sheppard Cl CW1	3 C1	Sycamore Cl CW5	12 D1
Sherborne Rd CW1	7 F4	Sycamore Gro CW11	4 D1
Sheridan Cl CW1	7 E1	Sydney Rd CW1	8 A4
Sheringham Dr CW1	7 E5		
Sherratt Cl CW5	12 D5	**Tabley** Cl CW11	4 B2
Sherwin St CW2	11 F2	Tabley Rd CW2	10 B1

Talbot Cl CW2	14 B2	Verity Cl CW1	8 C6
Talbot Way CW5	12 D5	Vernon Way CW1	3 C1
Tame Cl CW11	4 B1	Vicarage Gdns CW11	4 B1
Tanners Way CW5	12 B5	Vicarage La,	
Tarvin Av CW2	6 A6	Betchton CW11	5 G5
Tate Dr CW1	8 D6	Vicarage La,	
Tatton Dr CW11	5 E2	Elworth CW11	4 B2
Tatton Rd CW2	10 B2	Vicarage Rd CW1	8 D4
Taxmere Cl CW11	4 C2	Victoria Av, Crewe CW2	6 B6
Taylor Dr CW5	12 A3	Victoria Av,	
Telford Gdns CW11	4 C6	Haslington CW1	8 C6
Telford Pl CW5	12 A3	Victoria Centre CW2	**3 B1**
Tenchersfield CW5	12 D4	Victoria Mill Dr CW5	13 G3
Tennyson Cl CW2	10 C3	Victoria St, Crewe CW1	3 A2
Tennyson Dr CW1	7 H6	Victoria St,	
Thackery Ct CW11	4 A3	Sandbach CW11	4 D2
The Avenue CW11	4 B1	Villiers Russell Cl CW1	7 F5
The Barony		Vincent St CW1	7 H6
Employment Pk		Vine Tree Av,	
CW5	**12 C1**	Crewe CW2	11 E2
The Beeches CW5	12 C4	Vine Tree Av,	
The Birches CW2	11 F4	Shavington CW2	14 B1
The Blankeney CW5	12 C4	Volunteer Av CW5	12 C3
The Brambles CW1	8 C5	Volunteer Flds CW5	12 C3
The Broadway CW5	12 D3		
The Brooklands CW2	15 E3	**Waine** St CW1	7 G5
The Circle CW2	11 G3	Wakefield Cl CW1	6 C3
The Commons CW11	5 E2	Waldron Av CW1	16 D1
The Coppice CW11	4 B1	Waldron Gdns CW2	10 C3
The Crescent CW5	12 C3	Waldron Rd CW1	8 D6
The Dingle CW1	8 D4	Waldrons La CW1	7 F1
The Flds CW5	13 H4	Walford Av CW2	11 E1
The Gullet CW5	12 C3	Walker Cl CW1	8 D6
The Haven CW1	7 F3	Walker St CW1	7 E5
The Hill CW11	5 F3	Wall Fields Cl CW5	12 C2
The Oak Gro CW5	12 C6	Wall Fields Rd CW5	12 C2
The Orchards CW2	14 C2	Wall La CW5	12 B3
The Paddock CW5	13 G4	Wallis St CW1	3 C1
The Poplars CW2	10 C5	Walpole Cl CW1	8 C5
The Retreat CW1	7 F4	Walthall St CW2	3 A4
The Spinney,		Warburton Way*,	
Nantwich CW5	13 G2	Hightown CW11	5 E3
The Spinney,		Wareham Dr CW1	7 E2
Sandbach CW11	5 F3	Warrington Av CW1	7 E4
The Willows CW11	5 E2	Wasdale Gro CW1	7 E1
The Woodlands CW11	5 F4	Water Lode CW5	12 A3
Third Av, Crewe CW1	11 H3	Waterloo Rd CW1	8 D5
Third Av,		Waterside Mews CW11	4 C6
Sandbach CW11	4 D4	Waverton Cl CW1	6 A6
Thirlmere Rd CW2	10 C3	Waverton Cl CW4	16 E4
Thomas Av CW5	12 D5	Waybutt La CW2	15 H5
Thomas St CW1	3 C1	Weaver Bank CW5	12 B3
Thorley Gro CW2	10 D3	Weaver Cl CW11	4 B2
Thorn Tree Dr CW1	6 D1	Weaver Rd CW5	12 C3
Thornbrook Way CW11	4 A3	Weaverside CW5	12 C6
Thornton Dr CW2	10 D5	Well Bank CW11	5 E2
Thorpe Cl CW1	6 C2	Wellcroft Cl CW2	10 D5
Tilstone Cl CW2	15 E4	Welles St CW11	5 E2
Timbrell Av CW5	6 C4	Wellesley Av CW1	8 C6
Tinkersfield CW5	13 E5	Wellington Rd CW5	12 C4
Tiverton Cl CW11	5 F2	Wells Av CW1	8 D4
Tollemache Dr CW1	6 D2	Wellswood Dr CW2	10 C5
Tollitt St CW1	3 B2	Welsh Row CW5	12 A3
Tomkinson Cl CW1	6 C3	Welshmens La CW5	12 A1
Tommys La CW1	3 D5	Wesley Av CW11	5 E3
Tower Way CW1	3 B2	Wesley Cl CW5	12 C4
Towers Cl CW2	10 D5	Wesley Pl CW2	3 C5
Townfields CW11	4 D4	Wessex Cl CW2	14 C3
Trevithick Cl CW1	8 A6	West Av, Crewe CW1	7 E6
Tricketts La CW5	13 H3	West Av, Weston CW2	15 H1
Tricketts Mews CW5	13 H3	West St, Crewe CW1	3 A1
Trinity Cl CW2	10 D3	West St,	
Tudor Way CW5	12 B3	Haslington CW1	8 D5
Tunbridge Cl CW2	10 D4	West Way, Crewe CW2	14 D1
Turner St CW5	12 B3	West Way,	
Twemlow Av CW11	5 E1	Sandbach CW11	4 C5
Tyldesley Way CW5	12 A2	Westbourne Av CW1	6 D4
Tynedale Av CW2	3 A6	Westbury Cl CW1	11 E4
		Western Av CW5	12 C5
Ullswater Av CW2	10 B1	Westfield Dr CW2	10 B4
Underwood La CW1	6 D5	Westgate Pk CW2	15 E4
Union St, Crewe CW2	3 B5	Westholme Cl CW2	11 F4
Union St,		Westmere Cl CW2	15 H1
Sandbach CW11	4 D3	Westmere Dr CW1	16 A2
		Westminster St CW2	3 B5
Valebrook Dr CW5	14 A6	**Weston Centre CW1**	**11 H2**
Valley Rd CW2	10 C3	Weston Cl CW1	11 G2
Vauxhall Pl CW5	12 C1	Weston La CW2	14 C1
Vauxhall Rd CW5	12 C1	Weston Rd CW1	11 G2
Verdin Ct CW1	6 D2	Wharfdale Av CW5	7 E1
		Wheatley Rd CW1	7 H4

Wheelman Rd CW1	6 C3		
Wheelock By-Pass CW11	4 D6		
Wheelock Wharf CW11	4 D6		
Whirlow Rd CW2	10 D5		
Whitby Cl CW1	7 E2		
White Av CW2	6 C6		
White Hart La CW2	10 B4		
Whitehall Ct CW5	12 B3		
Whitehouse La CW5	12 D2		
Whites La CW2	16 B6		
Whitewell Cl CW5	12 D3		
Whitlow Av CW5	12 C4		
Whittaker Cl CW1	6 D3		
Wickstead Cl CW5	13 E4		
Wilderhope Cl CW2	11 E5		
Wilding St CW1	7 H6		
Willaston Hall Gdns			
CW5	13 G3		
William Foden Cl CW11	4 A2		
William Ho*,			
Princes Ct CW2	10 C1		
Willow Cres CW2	10 C2		
Willow Ct CW5	12 D2		
Willow Dr CW11	5 G2		
Willows Cl CW2	11 E5		
Windermere Rd CW2	10 B2		
Windsor Av, Crewe CW1	6 D3		
Windsor Av,			
Nantwich CW5	12 C5		
Wisdom Walk*,			
Eric Dr CW11	4 A2		
Wistaston Av CW2	10 C2		
Wistaston Green Rd			
CW2	10 A1		
Wistaston Pk CW2	10 C3		
Wistaston Rd,			
Crewe CW2	3 A3		
Wistaston Rd,			
Nantwich CW5	13 H3		
Wisterdale Cl CW2	10 D5		
Witham Cl CW2	10 D4		
Withington Cl CW11	5 F2		
Withnall Dr CW2	14 B2		
Woobank Cl CW2	10 D5		
Wood St CW2	3 C6		
Woodcote Pl CW11	9 F2		
Woodcott Cl CW2	15 E4		
Woodford Cl CW2	10 C2		
Woodland Av,			
Crewe CW1	8 A6		
Woodland Av,			
Nantwich CW5	12 D3		
Woodland Gdns CW1	7 G4		
Woodnoth Dr CW2	14 C1		
Woodside Av CW2	10 C3		
Woodside Dr CW11	5 F3		
Woodside La CW2	10 C3		
Woolston Dr CW2	15 E4		
Wordsworth Cl,			
Crewe CW2	10 C3		
Wordsworth Cl,			
Sandbach CW11	4 A3		
Wordsworth Dr CW1	7 H6		
Worthington Cl CW5	13 E4		
Wrenmere Cl CW11	4 B1		
Wright Ct CW5	12 D4		
Wrights La CW11	5 G3		
Wrinehill Rd CW5	14 B6		
Wybunbury La CW5	13 F5		
Wybunbury Rd CW5	13 H4		
Wyche Av CW5	12 B3		
Wyche Bank CW5	12 B3		
Yates St CW1	3 A6		
Yew Tree Dr CW5	12 B3		
Yew Tree Rd CW2	10 D4		
Zan Dr CW11	4 C6		
Zan Ind Pk CW11	4 D6		